THIS WALKER BOOK BELONGS TO:

gustav
moggol

*For Wally*

First published 1987 by Walker Books Ltd
87 Vauxhall Walk, London SE11 5HJ

This Special New Edition published 1997

2 4 6 8 10 9 7 5 3 1

© 1987, 1997 Martin Handford

The right of Martin Handford to be identified as author/illustrator
of this work has been asserted by him in accordance with the
Copyright, Designs and Patents Act 1988.

Printed in Hong Kong

British Library Cataloguing in Publication Data
A catalogue record for this book
is available from the British Library.

ISBN 0-7445-5536-1 (Hdbk)
ISBN 0-7445-5429-2 (Pbk)

# MARTIN HANDFORD

WALKER BOOKS
AND SUBSIDIARIES
LONDON • BOSTON • SYDNEY

HI FRIENDS!

MY NAME IS WALLY. I'M JUST SETTING OFF ON A WORLD-WIDE HIKE. YOU CAN COME TOO. ALL YOU HAVE TO DO IS FIND ME.

I'VE GOT ALL I NEED — WALKING STICK, KETTLE, MALLET, CUP, RUCKSACK, SLEEPING BAG, BINOCULARS, CAMERA, SNORKEL, BELT, BAG AND SHOVEL.

BY THE WAY, I'M NOT TRAVELLING ON MY OWN. WHEREVER I GO, THERE ARE LOTS OF OTHER CHARACTERS FOR YOU TO SPOT. FIRST FIND WOOF (BUT ALL YOU CAN SEE IS HIS TAIL), WENDA, WIZARD WHITEBEARD AND ODLAW. THERE ARE ALSO 25 WALLY-WATCHERS SOMEWHERE, EACH OF WHOM APPEARS ONLY ONCE ON MY TRAVELS. CAN YOU FIND ONE OTHER CHARACTER WHO APPEARS IN EVERY SCENE? ALSO IN EVERY SCENE, CAN YOU SPOT MY KEY, WOOF'S BONE, WENDA'S CAMERA, WIZARD WHITEBEARD'S SCROLL, AND ODLAW'S BINOCULARS?

WOW! WHAT A SEARCH! Wally

GREETINGS,
WALLY FOLLOWERS!
WOW, THE BEACH WAS
GREAT TODAY! I SAW
THIS GIRL STICK AN
ICE-CREAM IN HER
BROTHER'S FACE, AND
THERE WAS A SAND-
CASTLE WITH A REAL
KNIGHT IN ARMOUR
INSIDE! FANTASTIC!

Wally

TO:
WALLY FOLLOWERS,
HERE, THERE,
EVERYWHERE.

WHERE'S WALLY? DEPARTMENT STORE

WOTCHA, WALLY-WATCHERS!
SAW SOME TRULY TERRIFIC
SIGHTS TODAY – SOMEONE
BURNING TROUSERS WITH
AN IRON; A LONG THIN MAN
WITH A LONG THIN TIE;
A GLOVE ATTACKING A MAN.
PHEW! INCREDIBLE!

Wally

TO:
WALLY-WATCHERS,
OVER THE MOON,
THE WILD WEST,
NOW.

ROLL UP, WALLY FUN LOVERS!
WOW! I'VE LOST ALL MY
THINGS, ONE IN EVERY PLACE.
NOW YOU HAVE TO GO BACK
AND FIND THEM. AND
SOMEWHERE ONE OF THE
WALLY-WATCHERS HAS LOST
THE BOBBLE FROM HIS HAT.
CAN YOU SPOT WHICH ONE,
AND FIND THE MISSING
BOBBLE?

*Wally*

WHERE'S FAIRGROUND WALLY?

TO:
WALLY FUN LOVERS,
BACK TO THE BEGINNING,
START AGAIN,
TERRIFIC.

# THE GREAT WHERE'S WALLY? CHECKLIST
Hundreds more things for Wally-watchers to watch out for!

## IN TOWN
- A dog on a roof
- A man on a fountain
- A man about to trip over a dog's lead
- A car crash
- A keen barber
- People in a street, watching TV
- A puncture caused by a Roman arrow
- A tearful tune
- A boy attacked by a plant
- A waiter who isn't concentrating
- A robber who's been clobbered
- A face on a wall
- A man coming out of a man-hole
- A man feeding pigeons
- A bicycle crash

## SKI SLOPES
- A man reading on a roof
- A flying skier
- A runaway skier
- A backward skier
- A portrait in snow
- An illegal fisherman
- A snowball in the neck
- Two unconscious skiers
- Two skiers hitting trees
- An Alpine horn
- A snow skier
- A flag collector
- Two very scruffy skiers
- A skier up a tree
- A water skier on snow
- A Yeti
- A skiing reindeer
- A roof jumper
- A heap of skaters

## THE RAILWAY STATION
- A boy falling from a train
- A break-down on tracks
- Naughty children on a train roof
- People being knocked over by a door
- A man about to step on a ball
- Three different times at the same time
- A wheelbarrow pram
- A face on a train
- Five people reading one newspaper
- A struggling bag carrier
- A show-off with suitcases
- A man losing everything from his cases
- A smoking train
- A squeeze on a bench
- A dog tearing a man's trousers
- Fare dodgers
- A hand caught between doors
- A cattle stampede
- A man breaking a weighing machine

## ON THE BEACH
- A dog biting a boy's bottom
- A man who is overdressed
- A muscular medallion man
- A popular girl
- A water skier on water
- A stripy photo
- A punctured lilo
- A donkey who likes ice-cream
- A man being squashed
- A punctured beach ball
- A human pyramid
- A human stepping-stone
- Two odd friends
- A cowboy
- A human donkey
- Age and beauty
- A boy who follows in his father's footsteps
- Two men with vests, one without
- A boy being tortured by a spider
- A show-off with sandcastles
- A gang of hat robbers
- An Arab making pyramids
- Three protruding tongues
- Two oddly fitting hats
- An odd couple
- Five spiders
- A towel with a hole in it
- A punctured hovercraft
- A boy who's not allowed any ice-cream

## CAMP SITE
- A bull in a hedge
- Bull horns
- A shark in a canal
- A bull seeing red
- A careless kick
- Tea in a lap
- A low bridge
- People knocked over by a mallet
- A man surprised undressing
- A bicycle tyre about to be punctured
- Camper's camels
- A scarecrow that doesn't work
- A wigwam
- Large biceps
- A collapsed tent
- A smoking barbecue
- A fisherman catching old boots
- A winning penny-farthing
- Boy scouts making fire
- A roller hiker
- A man blowing up a boat
- A camper's butler
- Runners on the road
- A bull chasing children
- Scruffy campers
- Thirsty walkers

## SPORTS STADIUM
- Three pairs of feet, sticking out of sand
- A cowboy starting races
- Hopeless hurdlers
- Ten children with fifteen legs
- A record thrower
- A shot-put juggler
- An ear trumpet
- A vaulting horse
- A runner with two wheels
- A parachuting vaulter
- A Scotsman with a caber
- An elephant pulling a rope
- People being knocked over by a hammer
- A gardener
- Three frogmen
- A nude runner
- A bed
- A bandaged boy
- A runner with four legs
- A sunken jumper
- A man with an odd pair of legs
- A man chasing a dog, chasing a cat
- A boy squirting water

## MUSEUM

- A very big skeleton
- A clown squirting water
- A catapult firing a child
- A bird's nest in a woman's hair
- A highwayman
- A popping bicep
- An arrow in the neck
- A knight watching TV
- Picture robbers
- A smoking picture
- A leaking watercolour
- Fighting pictures
- A king and queen
- A fat picture and a thin one
- Three cave men
- A game of catch with a bomb
- Charioteers
- A collapsing pillar

## SAFARI PARK

- Noah's Ark
- A message in a bottle
- A hippo having its teeth cleaned
- A bird's nest in an antler
- A hungry giraffe
- An ice-cream robber
- A zebra crossing
- Father Christmas
- Three owls
- A unicorn
- Caged people
- A lion driving a car
- Bears
- Tarzan
- Lion cubs
- An Indian tiger
- Two queues for the toilets
- Animals' beauty parlour
- An elephant squirting water

## DEPARTMENT STORE

- An ironing demonstration
- A woman surprised undressing
- A man whose boots face the wrong way
- A man with heavy shopping
- A misbehaving vacuum cleaner
- Ties that match their wearers
- A man washing his clothes
- A man trying on a jacket that's too big
- A woman tripping over toys
- A boy pulling a girl's hair
- A boy riding in a shopping trolley
- A glove that's alive

## AT SEA

- A windsurfer
- A boat punctured by an arrow
- A sword fight with a swordfish
- A school of whales
- Seasick sailors
- A leaking diver
- A boat crash
- A bathtub
- A seabed
- A game of noughts and crosses
- A lucky fisherman
- Three lumberjacks
- Unlucky fishermen
- Two water skiers in a tangle
- Fish robbers
- A sea cowboy
- A fishy photo
- A man being strangled by an octopus
- Stowaways
- A Chinese junk
- A wave at sea

## FAIRGROUND

- A cannon at a rifle range
- A bumper car run wild
- A sword swallower
- A one-armed bandit
- A flying balloon seller
- A runaway fairground rocket
- A runaway fairground horse
- A haunted house
- Seven lost children and a lost dog
- A tank crash
- A weightlifter dropping his weights
- Three clowns
- Three men dressed as bears

## AIRPORT

- A flying saucer
- A boy who's been hiding in a suitcase
- A child firing a catapult
- A leaking fuel pipe
- Flight controllers playing badminton
- A rocket
- A turret
- Three watch smugglers
- Naughty children on a plane
- A forklift truck
- A wind-sock
- A chopper
- A plane that doesn't fly
- A flying Ace
- Dracula
- Five men blowing up a balloon
- Runners on a runaway
- Four smoking people
- Four people falling from a plane
- A cargo of cattle
- A fire engine
- Three childish pilots
- An airship being punctured

## WOW! WHAT A SEARCH!

Did you find Wally, all his friends, and all the things they lost? Did you find the one scene where Wally and Odlaw both lost their binoculars? Odlaw's binoculars are the ones nearest to him. Did you find the extra character who appears in every scene? If not, keep looking! Wow! Fantastic!

# THE WHERE'S WALLY? BOOKS
## by Martin Handford

### WHERE'S WALLY?

The book that started it all. Wally wanders across a crowded beach, ski-slope, safari park…

"Hours of eye-boggling entertainment." *The Mail on Sunday*

0-7445-5429-2   £5.99

### WHERE'S WALLY NOW?

Wally hikes his way through history, dropping books as he goes. Find him among the gladiators of Ancient Rome, pirates, vikings, crusaders, cowboys…

"A book which almost defies description… It is a fun book, often hilarious."
*Times Educational Supplement*

0-7445-5443-8   £5.99

### WHERE'S WALLY? 3 THE FANTASTIC JOURNEY

Wally journeys to the realms of fantasy. Find him among gobbling gluttons, nasty nasties, dwarves, knights, giants…

"Children of all ages, mums and dads too, will relish *Where's Wally? 3 The Fantastic Journey*… Its intricately detailed pictures guarantee hours of pleasure." *Susan Hill, Today*

0-7445-5444-6   £5.99

### WHERE'S WALLY? IN HOLLYWOOD

Wally goes on a spectacular tour of Tinseltown. Find Wally and his friends on the crowded sets of silent movies, musicals, westerns, swashbuckling adventures, epics…

"Wonderful." *The Observer*

0-7445-5445-4   £5.99

### WHERE'S WALLY? THE ULTIMATE FUN BOOK

Puzzles, press-outs, stickers, games, teasers… Wow! Amazing! The ultimate in fun! Don't miss it!

0-7445-1704-4   £4.99

### WHERE'S WALLY? THE MAGNIFICENT POSTER BOOK

The greatest poster book of the century: wall-to-wall Wally! A breath-taking poster collection of favourite pictures and new ones, including the amazing Where's Wally in the Land of Sport! It's truly magnificent!

0-7445-1944-6   £8.99

### WHERE'S WALLY? STICKER BOOKS

Each of these books has over 250 full-colour stickers, plus a large background picture, so that Wally-watchers can make their own eye-boggling scenes!

WHERE'S WALLY? THE DAZZLING DEEP-SEA DIVERS STICKER BOOK
0-7445-3615-4   £3.99

WHERE'S WALLY? THE FABULOUS FLYING CARPETS STICKER BOOK
0-7445-3616-2   £3.99

**Walker Paperbacks are available from most booksellers, or by post from B.B.C.S., P.O. Box 941, Hull, North Humberside HU1 3YQ**
**24 hour telephone credit card line 01482 224626**

To order, send: Title, author, ISBN number and price for each book ordered, your full name and address, cheque or postal order payable to BBCS for the total amount and allow the following for postage and packing:
UK and BFPO: £1.00 for the first book, and 50p for each additional book to a maximum of £3.50.
Overseas and Eire: £2.00 for the first book, £1.00 for the second and 50p for each additional book.

Prices and availability are subject to change without notice.